"Zack Rawsthorne skewers political correctness with a deft hand, exposing the hypocrisy and detachment of the left with humor."
--Thomas Lifson,
Editor, American Thinker

ZACK RAWSTHORNE

"...Laura Ingraham loved your picture for her... great stuff, I am a huge fan... the [Ronald Reagan Black Tie/Blue Jeans] event went really well, and your [drawing] was a great success... 1000 people or more were there including the Governor, Senate President, Speaker of the House and others..."
--Stafford Jones,
Republican Party Chairman, FL

"...like Charles Addams meets P.J. O'Rourke... hilarious, timeless material."
--Dr. Paul Ibbetson,
'The Conscience of Kansas' Radio Show
Author, Lecturer, Fmr. Chief of Police

"Excellent cartoons... keep them coming."
--Van Helsing,
Creator, Moonbattery.com

"I have found Zack Rawsthorne's political cartoons to be absolutely refreshing... Zack is by far the most talented cartoonist that I know of. I am honored to be associated with him."
--Keith D. Sellars,
Web-Based Media Consultant
Republican Party Chairman

"Permit me to praise your work, which is SUPER..."
--Bill Rolen,
Editor in Chief, The Citizens Informer
Republican Party Delegate

"...Awesome... brilliant."
--Tom Mannis,
Advertising, Publishing & Marketing
Chicago News Bench

"Zack Rawsthorne is a superb humorist! His political cartoons are witty and spot on."
--Andie Brownlow,
Conservative Writer

"...pulls the carpet out from under New Liberalism with subtle grace...defeats postmodernism with profound irony."
--D.A.,
Lt. Cmdr., USNR

"Anything that makes a conservative laugh and a liberal cringe--- is a good thing."

--L. Brent Bozell III,
President and Founder
Media Research Center

ZACK RAWSTHORNE

"*Diversity Lane* is marvelous. Rawsthorne's characters are drawn with great delicacy... simple lines combined with a deft use of washes. The spaces they inhabit are always perfectly composed...but it's the expressive power of his characters that is most dazzling, from Diversity's sneers of utter contempt to Devon's NPR snootiness -- that's why this spot-on depiction of a liberal household takes flight. It is rare to find someone who can draw so well, and yet still be this funny."

--John Morra,
Internationally Renowned Painter

"Zack is right on target and I am more than appreciative of him and his work... one gutsy cartoonist."

--Dr. Rick W.,
Ret. U.S. Army Aviator

"Laugh-out-loud scenes of the most outrageously stereotypical PC "family unit" ever... some of the best political/social commentary out there... if you appreciate a stinging, spot-on sense of timing, read this book."

--Larry Melton,
Teacher, Christian Private School

"You are a genius!"

--Sharon Graham Doyle,
Legal Secretary/Administrative Assistant

"A witty and pithy critique of the generation that never grew-up (as seen by their children)... beautifully rendered."

--Craig Maxwell,
Bookseller, Maxwell's House of Books

"Fantastic, love it... thanks for the laughs."

-Ron Clendening,
Professional Geologist

"I have long been a fan of the obvious professional quality of Zack's cartoons... visually, a feast of brilliant 3D detail... politically, a direct hit on left-wing foolishness..."

--Jose Reyes,
Editor, Cubanology.com

"...it's good to see a political cartoon from a conservative viewpoint that's clever and funny..."
--Andrew L.,
Computer Programmer

"I think your work is a national treasure…"

--Kevin Lamb,
Managing Editor,
The Social Contract

ZACK RAWSTHORNE

"…Gripping medicine that, even for an independent like me, is fashioned to go down easy. Almost as importantly, your cartoons are fun! Quality worthy of *The New Yorker*…"

--Lynn M.,
Editor/Small Business Owner

"…Pure comic genius…gawd I heart you…"

--SondraK,
SondraK.com
Caregiver

"…love your work… I'll put [your book] next to my Bloom County and P.J. O'Rourke tomes."

--Mark Comstock,
Technical Writer

"Brilliantly pokes fun at the foibles of the liberal left...."

--Jess Peterson,
Photographer

"You are really good… we need to get you famous…"

--Christopher Cook,
President and Founder,
Modern Conservative and AnyStreet.org.

"…a slamdunk …just flippin' brilliant. Great symbolic detail… Sharp and pointed and all too true."

--Wesley M.,
inmycopiousfreetime.blogspot.com

"If he were any wittier he'd have to draw slower."

--Wayne Seguin,
Republican Candidate,
County Commissioner

"…your wonderful cartoons should be seen by the whole world…"

--Z,
gollygeez.blogspot.com

"Diversity Lane is an outstanding depiction of the absurdity of the PC mentality."

–Melek,
Freedom Advocate, SC

rsity NE **

amily Saga

ZACK RAWSTHORNE

Dedication

For my parents, with gratitude
for raising me to have good sense.
Or giving it their best shot, anyway.

and

To the United States Armed Forces,
whose steadfast sacrifice and protection
of our nation
ensures us all the liberty to live, write,
and draw funny pictures
in blessed peace and freedom.

! NOTICE OF ERROR !
Somewhere within these pages is a visual error: a conservative
element has managed to slip into the leftwing carnival of the mind
known as the Lane household. And it's up to you, sharp reader, to spot it.
First visual sleuth to email in the correct faux pas (to zackrawsthorne@cox.net)
will win a magnificently framed, hand signed original drawing
from Diversity Lane and have your name and the solution
announced at the website & the blog:
www.diversitylane.com and www.diversitylane.wordpress.com
NOTE: Please do not send us attachments.

First published by Dog Ear Publishing
4010 W. 86th Street, Ste H
Indianapolis, IN 46268
www.dogearpublishing.net

ISBN: 978-160844-884-5

This book is a work of fiction. Places, events, and situations in this book are purely fictional
and any resemblance to actual persons, living or dead, is coincidental.

This paper is acid free and meets all ANSI standards for archival quality paper.
Printed in the United States of America

Denunciation

For the American mainstream media.

When Walter Duranty, then New York Times Moscow correspondent,
patently denied to the world via his esteemed newspaper the (by then obvious) existence of Stalin's imposed
Ukrainian famine (quite a denial, since 25,000 a day were dropping dead at the
time), some twisted convoluted lightbulb apparently popped up over the heads of all the muckety-mucks at
the NYTimes—possibly an early CFL bulb?-- because the "Reportorial Untruth On Behalf of Leftism"
template stuck and the cheery Parade of Dishonesty has marched on right up to the present.

Why did mainstream TV News, supposed purveyors of Truth-- I'm laughing as I type that--
take around *two weeks* to report on ClimateGate (i.e., the revelation that climate scientists colluded to hide
the *decline* in global temperatures)? Answer: because the details of the scandal totally contradicted their
adoringly cherished Global Warming model. So-called 'conservative' talk radio
reported on it immediately, as did Fox News.
Where were you guys?

Then there's the one about the ACORN tapes, where filmmakers James O'Keefe and Hannah
Giles, posing as a pimp and prostitute (call them P & P for short) secretly videotaped ACORN employees at
a number of different ACORN offices instructing the P & P team how to falsify tax forms for 13 "very young"
girls from El Salvador whom P & P pretended they wanted to import into child prostitution. I mean, I don't
care if ACORN *is* Obama's favorite community organizing group, this is a form of community organizing that
just isn't done. The exposé-videos were falling down like acorns from an oak tree that summer but the
mainstream press sat on the story *for days* after sources like talk radio and Fox were all over it. Had the
sleazy hooker-pump been on the other foot, i.e. if it was the NRA or some conservative group that had been
exposed, Big News would have kick-started a whole new channel to plaster the story over the airwaves with
24/7. So again: *Where were you guys?*

(It's like some kind of old '60s folksong:
"Child prostitution-rings/ Where were you?
Ukrainian genocide/ Where were you?
Global Warming cover-ups/ Where were you?
O, man, where were you?...")

Examples like these are not rare, they're constant, and I could continue and fill this whole book
with accounts of your cartoonish impersonations of journalism but I have other cartoons to get to; readers
who want more like this need only compare the day to day left-slant of Big Media to the well-documented,
clearly elucidated facts as generally presented on those scary right wing Fonts of Evil, the internet, talk radio
and Fox News. To sum up, I offer a friendly suggestion. Instead of pretending to be engaging in journalism,
a charade about as convincing to the informed among us as a couple 6-year-olds playing at Cowboys and
Indians, why not just come out and cheer honestly for your team? Here's a freebie for you to use in the
2012 election:

He's our guy! He's our man!
Go Obama, Yes We Can!
We got strength! We got might!
Lefties, lefties, fight, fight, fight!"

(Pom-poms can be easily acquired via many sources on the World Wide Web.)

O, that way madness lies; let me shun that;
No more of that.

--*Shakespeare,*
King Lear
Act 3, Scene 4

TABLE OF CONTENTS

Thanks

A special thanks goes out to Maxwell's House of Books (maxwellshouseofbooks.com), a dealer in fine used books and my favorite online source for reading material. Whether extending a must-read suggestion while taking a phoned-in order or passing along a thought-provoking concept from C. S. Lewis or Harry V. Jaffa, here is a venue where erudition and patriotism still live.

I'd also like to thank the authors, educators, talk show hosts, journalists and assorted communicators who've helped influence me away from the politically conformist world-view of the dominant culture. If this nation is to be saved from the dry rot of neurotic self-doubt and decline it's in large part to these warriors in words that we'll owe our gratitude. Of current writers some of my favorites (in no particular order) are Victor Davis Hanson, Thomas Sowell, Charles Krauthammer, Mark Steyn, Linda Chavez, George Will, Ann Coulter, Peter Wehner, Dinesh D'Souza, Andrew McCarthy, Mark Levin, Steven Emerson, Michelle Malkin, Jonah Goldberg, Shelby Steele, Mona Charen, Dorothy Rabinowitz and Theodore Dalrymple but there are of course numerous other outstanding writers I read regularly. Of the talkers (often fine writers as well) I've benefited over the years from listening to Barry Farber, Bob Grant, Dennis Prager, Rush Limbaugh, Laura Ingraham, Mark Levin, Larry Elder, Al Rantel, Sean Hannity, Mike Gallagher, Michael Medved, Tammy Bruce, Jeff Kuhner, Roger Hedgecock, Hugh Hewitt and Monica Crowley though again there are a number of other extraordinary communicators out there. Derided by a largely under-educated mainstream culture as (at best) "mere" conservative authors or "mere" talk show hosts, the above individuals and others in their field turn out on extended examination to be-- despite the occasionally confrontational style—thoughtful, ultra-informed professionals who tower over the often mundane talents of the more "acceptable" thinkers, writers and news personalities prescribed for us by the mainstream culture. Further: their oft-touted "scary right-wing bent" turns out under scrutiny to be essentially a font of common sense and the benign, classically American values of the Founders of our country; while the all-pervasive mainstream-media opiners from Hollywood to Manhattan to Washington emerge under objective examination as increasingly and dangerously left-leaning. Any honest reader or listener will find this to be true, if only he will be courageous enough to ignore the baleful admonitions of the In Crowd and expose himself with real objectivity to the views of the other side for a relatively short period of time.

And thanks also are due to the many talented writers associated with blogs or websites whose efforts in a worthy cause, as well as personal words of encouragement, have been a source of inspiration. These include (with www.s deleted for easier reading): americanthinker.com, conservababes.com, chadkentspeaks.com, cubanology.com, faultlineusa.blogspot.com, forthardknox.com, gollygeez.blogspot.com, hopeandchangecartoons.blogspot.com, lbbetsonusa.blogtownhall.com, inmycopiousfreetime.blogspot.com, iowntheworld.com, kyleanneshiver.com, laurichg.blogspot.com, letterstoliberals.blogspot.com, makalakapisei.blogspot.com, mattveasey.com, moonbattery.com, politicalbyline.com, republicaninthearts.blogspot.com, saberpoint.com, scottthong.wordpress.com, shotinthedark.com, sondrak.com, thesocialcontract.com, thesteadyconservative.com/wordpress, vocalminority.typepad.com, wakepedia.blogspot.com, and wholereason.com. My apologies to those I may have overlooked.

DIVERSITY LANE

8-year-old daughter of Alex and Allison Lane

Well-grounded child who, thanks to liberal/left parents, endures a psychological environment about as reassuring as the Twilight Zone. Doesn't consider it a normal day till she's been accused of racism at least once; pays charitable visits to a local mental institution for balance.

ALLISON LANE

Wife of Alex/ gay partner of Devon/ ex-partner of Sierra/ mother of Diversity and Jayson

Elementary school teacher who hasn't cracked a math or history book in twenty years, preferring an intuitive approach. Holds advanced degrees in Politically Correct Linguistics, Radical Epistomology and Feminist Deconstructivist something.

SIERRA

Allison's ex/ currently claims various ethereal beings as partners

Gives the impression of someone who got stuck in a turnstyle in Sedona and couldn't get out. Owns more crystals than Obama has czars; subject to absentmindedness & drug-inspired accidents as she endeavors to make her way through a multidimensional reality.

CHARACTERS

ALEX LANE

Husband of Allison/ father of Diversity and Jayson

ACLU attorney; happy to be a cog in the wheel of the Left as it pursues its remorseless drive to remake America into something *good* for a change. A kind of socialist Captain Ahab, obsessed by his vision of an angry, bigoted nation despite stats, logic and objective observation to the contrary.

DEVON

Gay live-in partner of Allison

Angry lesbian leftist/feminist/activist whose every waking moment has political ramifications. Believes everything ought to be equal to everything else and won't be happy till it is. Turns out treatises on Autonomist Marxist Anarchism like they were pancakes.

JAYSON LANE

6-year-old son of Alex and Allison Lane

Raised like a twisted orchid in the leftist hothouse which is the Lane home, where religion & patriotism have been carefully weeded out; is thus in danger of becoming the perfect Progressive child. Goes to bed weeping each night in fear of Global Warming thanks to parental propagandizing that would have made Stalin proud.

1.

FROM WITHIN THE MADHOUSE

You hear about these things but you never think it'll happen in *your* neighborhood.

Eek! A flag!

Which sort of day does it feel like to you?

Wow, I had no idea your parents were so heavy into beauty pageants!

Whaddya mean you don't know how to handle it? Report the white racist bastard to the feds as an obvious domestic terrorist, and invite the Muslim gentleman in to compassionately discuss the issues troubling him!

We're teaching them to combat the hatemongers on the Right.

When will you *stop victimizing this defenseless child??*

I do think the town square looks 'sweet,' Jayson;
I'm just concerned about the lack of diversity.

They both picked the same *Che!* top to wear to
the Obama rally and neither one'll give an inch.

Which is worse: getting waterboarded or having to listen to them all night arguing about the dialectics of radical feminism?

We need to start talking about cutting back on train runs, Jayson--
there's Global Warming to think about now.

Look at that filthy racist cop: acting like those guys
are criminals just 'cause they're black...

Well, I'm not sure *I'm* okay with terrorists in her background.
We're hiring a babysitter here, not just a president.

Yes, I see the church. What I *don't* see is a *mosque...*

The karma around your toy village was like
totally horrendous. I've fixed it now...

Of course you can have the money for that toy lion, honey! This is a compassionate home, and I'm a compassionate mommy!

Look, I'll give it to you straight: we're not hiring someone based on
the content of their character, we're hiring someone based on
the color of their skin.

2.

HE *WON'T SHUT UP*

22

23

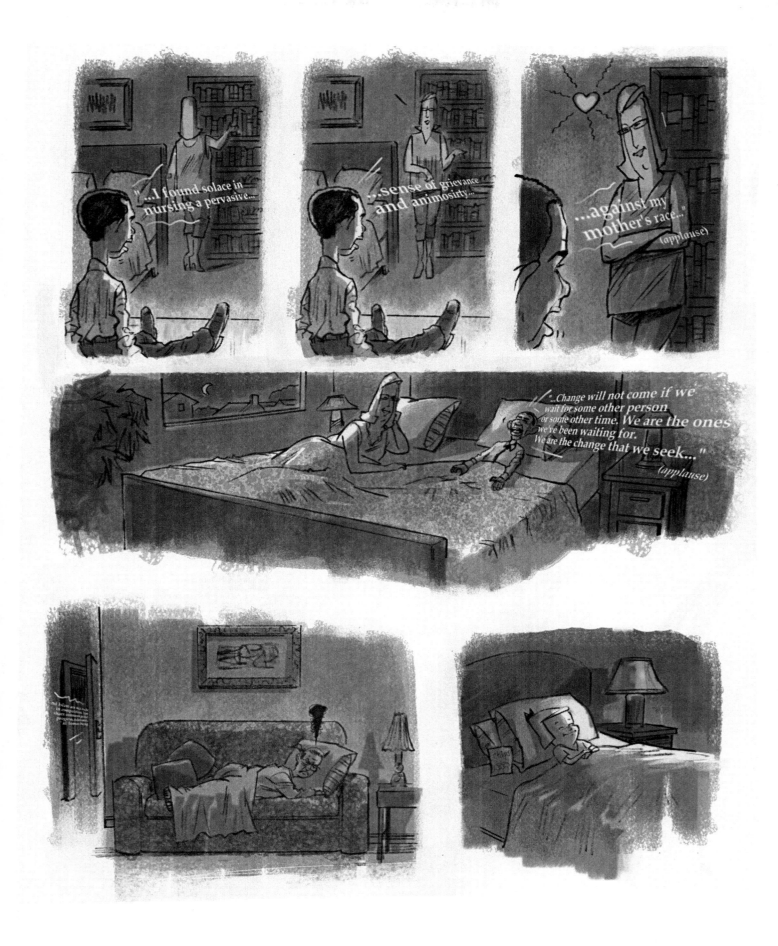

3.

DEVON VS REALITY

NO cars overturned! NO smashed windows! No grafitti, no police reports and no injuries! They call *that* a protest??

I'm fine with Jayson wanting to be a girl; why does he have to be *this* kind of girl?

Why no African-American husband for your Barbi? Do you have a latent unexpressed hostility toward dolls of color?

Who do we blame for this one-- Islamophobia in the Army
or America's violent right-wing culture?

If you comb that doll's hair one more time today I'm going to
take it in the backyard and burn it.

...I'm just saying to watch your step. Carbon dioxide's been identified
as a serious cause of Global Warming; that means if you were to
somehow *stop breathing* it could be defended as a net gain to the planet.

You call *that* a woman?

How do you cope with the total lack of diversity in her doll collection?

Gather round for popcorn, folks-- the America In Decline special's starting.

4.

PLAYMATES/
PROGRESSIVE AND NON-PROGRESSIVE

I don't *have* a Barbi's Dreamhouse anymore. Devon made me give it away
because if I kept it that would mean I was a materialist capitalist pig.

I know what you mean about this gloomy cloud cover.
Seems like it's been hanging over us for years!

He's only mean to people who treat *him* mean! With me it'll be *different!*

Jayson, this is LaDuayne, the new African-American boy from down the block.
I think he looks like a perfectly *fine* new friend for you and Diversity!

Okay, here's how I understand it. Allison and Alex are my bio-parents,
but then Allison discovered her androcentrism. So she married Mommy Sierra
and they both lived with Alex in a progressive post-patriarchal arrangement
until Sierra moved to Berkeley to find her inner child. Then Allison met Devon
who was just coming down from her existential crisis and they *all* moved to Berkeley.
And then one of them had Jayson but I can't remember which.

The one about the handsome king who saves the land from the rising ocean isn't in those. That one's supposed to be *real*.

Jayson! Come down from there right now and stop provoking LaDuayne!

When are they gonna build one that washes away the liberalism?

I don't even *like* you. I'm only playing with you 'cause you're black
and Allison says I have a *quota* to meet.

I can't really *explain* why I don't like her. It's just this *feeling* I've had for a while.

It's just like Obama! A great big shiny puffed-up balloon
with everyone's hopes and prayers riding on it-- but then
when it finally deflates and hits the ground
there's not a damn thing inside!

I don't mind her going off to Spain.
My beef is that she insisted on coming back.

I can't play with you anymore. My dad found out your parents listen to Mark Levin.

No-- this time *you* be the CIA and *I'll* be al Qaeda.
I'm *tired* of always being the bad guy.

Oh-- we have to check with *them* if we want to switch from Tag
to Freeze Tag. My playtime has been fully Centralized now.

Tell them it's a chihuahua that came over with a Mexican illegal.
It's your only shot at keeping it.

It's not an "illegal act," it's an *undocumented acquisition,*
and if you make a big fuss about it it means you're a ***nazi.***

*...and don't come back till you've brought home
a **Latina** friend for dinner.*

No *way* she counts as real Latina! Her parents
are *loaded*... and **Republican.**

No *wonder* we keep getting stuck with icky words!
It's **Obama** Scramble!

5.

THEY ALL WANT TO BE FRENCH

He'd *kill* to be French.

She says if *she* can't be French at least her livingroom can.

It's like some horrible creeping fungus that spreads a little every day.

Don't they ever get their berets mixed up?

*Just because you've become French doesn't mean
you can cook, paint or look good in Chanel.*

Even their buildings look like wine bottles...

At this point I'm thinking exorcism.

6.

BEYOND THE WALLS OF THE ASYLUM

Mommy, Mommy I don't *want* one!

Nope-- no big, greedy, overbearing corporation
for me, Anne-- I'm happy over at my government position!

Oh, don't mind them-- it's just their idea of how to throw
a welcoming party for the new Muslim family down the block.

Aren't they the coolest? I'm seeing victimizaton
in places I never dreamed it existed!

Put down the club, dear-- we want to avoid any aggressive behavior
which could impede patient dialog and negotiation.

Border of Mexico? Sure-- just turn left
at that next big butte and follow the bullet-ridden bodies.

"It was dreamt up and built by a megalomaniac and the U.S. government, wasted an ungodly amount of time and money, and was too big to be practical from the getgo." Sound familiar?

...and you're certain there won't be any of...*them* buried here?

It's okay Sierra hon', we've all made the same mistake. I once brought
an Elect Barney Frank sign to a Save The Whales demonstration!

'Out of business' is so negative. I'd prefer you
to call them 'post-commercial contingencies.'

Let's face it, we're *all* afraid to ask whether it's important art
or just some junk the janitor left behind.

Who would even *wanna* win this crappy thing?

They're rich/ we're poor/ they owe us. Just pop it in the bag if you like it--
think of it as helping the Government do it's work.

"Terrorist?" What are you talking about? I'm reporting him
for emitting environmentally unfriendly toxins
into the ecosystem!

7.

HELP– I CAN'T FIND MY 7TH CHAKRA

--Because she has no *home* anymore, *that's* why we're taking her in!
For two years her activist group's been lobbying to get a wind farm built,
not realizing her lot was in the middle of the development zone!

Never fall asleep in a Chippewa sweat lodge during a dream-catcher ceremony.

Allison, have you seen my jump rope? I can't find it *anywhere!*

I was about to split when I got into this major meditation on Barack.
I think I'm about to enter an altered state!

THE GREAT
CAPTION CONTEST

Open to everybody! --like Obamacare
except that it won't undermine your health!

Exciting awards to the winner!

Much of Sierra's history is shrouded in a haze
of pot smoke and incense vapors, which may account for
the disappearance of the original caption for this drawing.
You can help by emailing your best creative & funny caption
to zackrawsthorne@cox.net

10 best captions (and their authors) will be announced
at the Diversity Lane blog and the Diversity Lane website

www.diversitylane.wordpress.com (blog)   www.diversitylane.com (website)

Winner for top caption will be announced at both sites
and will receive a signed, framed set of original Diversity Lane drawings,
plus the honor of having their caption attached to
this drawing *for all eternity*

One submission per reader, please!
Sorry, no attachments with your emails

Sierra calling-- *from the hospital.* They stuck to schedule and held the
End Global Warming Rally in spite of the blizzard
and now she's got Chanting Pneumonia.

They've been playing on the wrong gameboard all afternoon
but they're both too stoned to figure it out.

She keeps channeling dead Republicans and it's driving her out of her gourd.

When you were a stupid teenager you rooted for the Black Panthers. Now you're a stupid 50-year-old and you're rooting for Code Pink. You oughta be horsewhipped from here to Bastogne...

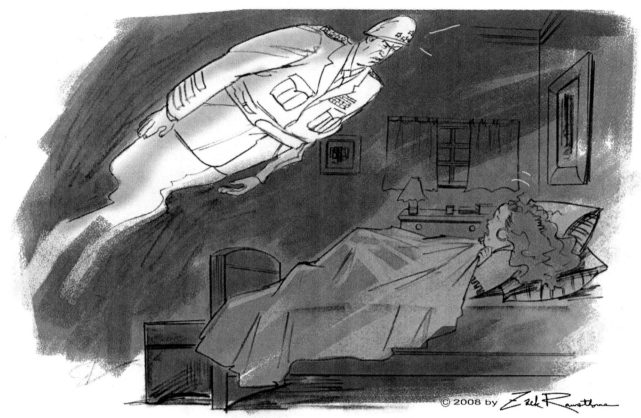

You're real down on the cops, the military, the church, the Boy Scouts.
Any upholders of simple decency that you *don't* hate, you ignorant witch?

She fell asleep channelling Patton and now he's loose in the house!

The Unicorn Shoppe, and hurry-- we're talkin' *bigtime* crystal withdrawal.

There I am-- stoned, half-naked and covered in mud at Woodstock.
...sigh... Those were the days!

Of course it's good for you! I've been eating it for years, and look at me!

8.

SCENES FROM AN ADOPTION

A MULTICULTURAL TRAGEDY

They're calling Angelina and Brad a 'rainbow family spreading multicultural inspiration everywhere.' Ever get the feeling you've missed the Progressive boat?

Isn't that a wee bit premature?

*The Clanahans just took in **handicapped Chinese twins** for chrissake and what do we got? **Two boring white kids.***

Did it ever occur to you that maybe we can't **afford** to be a rainbow family spreading multicultural inspiration everywhere?

Diversity's best friend Promethea: she's black, she's orphaned and she's available.
Can you imagine the Progressive street-cred we'd pick up off of this?

No really, I think it's *super* that they might adopt you! I'm just saying
there could be worse things in this world than life in an orphanage.

I told them during the adoption interview that I like Duke Ellington, Beethoven and Kelly Clarkson and my favorite book is Pride & Predjudice. How come all they want to get me is stereotypical black ghetto stuff? It's like they don't want me to be who I am...

They don't want any *part* of you unless it conforms to the rulebook of the Democrat Party. Face it: the only reason they adopted you is so you'll feel all grateful to them, buy into their crappy ideas today and vote for their crappy candidates tomorrow.

*You had her all morning at Love Me Yoga and **you** took her to the Vegan-Go-Round twice this week! When do **I** get to be seen with her?*

It's disgusting. We load up her room with the most progressive African-American culture we can find and what does she pick up to read? *Jane Austen.*

Take it you idiot! Can't you act like an African-American is supposed to act just once??

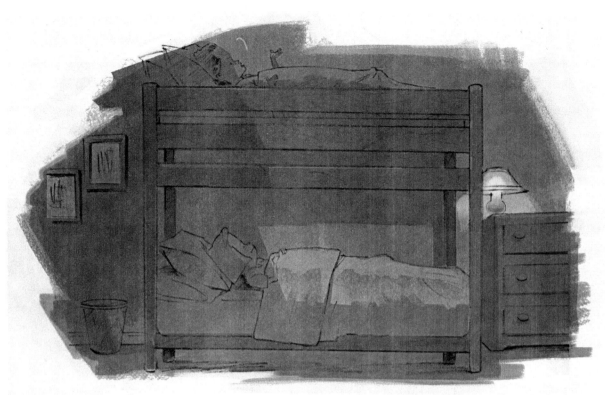

...and if they tell me one more time that I'm a victim
and can't make it without them I think I'll puke...

I tried to tell you about them before they took you in. They're just a new kind of racist
but with fancier footwork. The last thing they want is for you to exert any
self-reliance, strength or individuality: that would crush their beliefs
about how minorities are supposed to think, act and vote. Once you start thinking
outside the Democrat box you're dogmeat to them.

What do you mean you don't wanna go to a rap concert? **How can you not??**

...never been so embarassed in my life! You tell LaShonda Williams you **don't like Barack??**

We adopted you so you'd think like we do-- not go all independent-minded on us.
A few more weeks of you and we'd be the laughingstock of the Progressive community...

I know you needed a family... you just don't need *this* family.

Even if I was in the market for a kid and you were available I'd never adopt you.

9.

WE'RE *MELTING...* MELTING...

Well of *course* it's a sign of global warming!

I'm thinking if we can find the right angle
we could try to pin it on Climate Change.

See what I mean? They're *definitely warmer* this year.

Now see what you've done?

Excuse me, sir-- can you direct me to the Global Warming Symposium? Sir?

If global warming is so-o-o horrible,
how come they're not happy that it's all kinda fizzling out?

Wow! What kind of SUV causes THAT??

It's Sierra-- mild heart attack. She left the tub running, got stoned,
then saw water pooling down the hall and thought
the oceans were rising.

When does Rod Serling show up to explain it all to us?

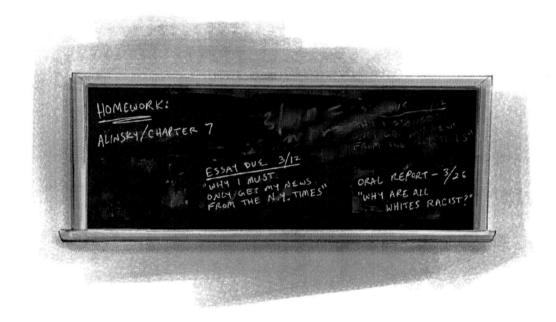

10.

EDUCATION & RE-EDUCATION

It's a *new* kind of hopscotch where nobody has to lose and feel marginalized.

Look, you're his teacher, you tell *me* how to turn him off!

...so we've eliminated Tag because it privileges bullies and Softball because it victimizes the skill-challenged. That leaves us with Study Hall and Let's Be Flowers. Everyone down with this?

...I know... I think it's disgusting that students
were allowed to opt out of Barack's address. Just more of
the usual close-minded, strong-armed partisanship from the other side...

So maybe it *is* a little premature. I can dream, can't I?

11.

WARNING: PROLONGED CHANTING
MAY LEAD TO CONFUSION

Uh-oh. Looks like Sierra has a new hobby.

As I understand it it's a mixture of pantheism, wiccan, paganism
and everything else they could find that wasn't Christian.

Welcome to the God of the Month club.

Can she maybe stop being a PanWiccan for like *five minutes?*

'What do they believe in?' What *don't* they believe in!

They say it's their religion and they'll drag in any damn ritual they *wanna* drag in.

Hey, I like ugly gods as much as anybody but we gotta draw a line *somewhere.*

Can't they ever get together without burning something?

12.

WE ARE THE PEOPLE WE'VE BEEN WAITING FOR

Just **look** how the rightwing mainstream media
sets it up so McCain looks like the underdog.

Y'know...even for me this one might be a bit much.

Awesome miniseries about the Third Reich last night. Just *imagine* a country
where your every thought is shaped by this all pervasive opinion-making *machine!*

Just keep telling them that *Change* is coming to your room.
You might not have to actually *do anything.*

I don't get it. It's like, who *doesn't* have friends who want to bomb the Pentagon?

I'm seeing it! I'm seeing it! You guys were right! O... B... A... M...

KIDS' → KORNER

Make your way home to safety
through the dangerous maze of
American Leftism! Make sure
you steer clear of:
* Obama's Appeasement Alley
* Devon's Den of Moral Relativism
* The Left Turn to Nowhere
* Wind Turbine Way
* The Valley of Victimhood
* Che's Cul-de-Sac
* Negativity Newstand

Get home safe?
Congratulations! You have
courage and common sense!

START

HOME

13.

MESSIAH LITE

It's still a white racist country; they've just found a new way to disguise it.

That one isn't a monument-- it's a pile of trash from the crowd on the National Mall.

I think this means that under Obamacare if they accidentally remove your colon instead of your appendix they can still give the operation a 'thumbs up.'

Can't he stay out of *anything?*

Remember the good old days, when press conferences didn't look like the PTL Club?

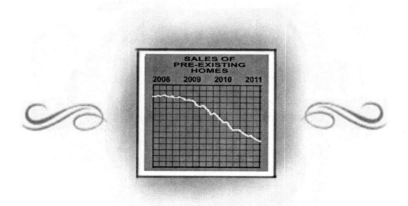

Leave it to Teddy...

No, *I* don't think he's overexposed. Do *you* think he's overexposed?

Ever have some friend that you *kinda* liked drop by to play...
and then you couldn't wait for them to leave... but they wouldn't?

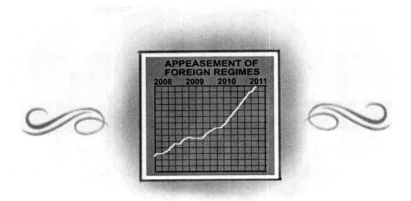

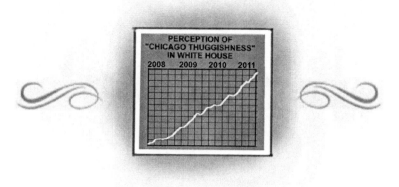

Why didn't he just go all the way and plow them into the buildings?
He's done pretty much everything else to us.

I'd say 83% is a *plenty* impressive amount, honey!
Why, is that what you got on your spelling quiz?

No I'm *not* upset over losing Michael Jackson! I'm upset over losing *America!*

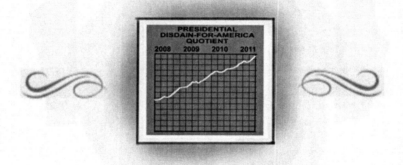

Maybe he'd work up a little more involvement with Afghanistan
if they'd put in a really sweet golf course?

The Wolf in Sheep's Clothing-- again? Why do you
always want me to read *that* story, honey?

Mother Teresa a "favorite philosopher?" Isn't Barack
vetting these people at *all??*

...and bless Mommy, and Daddy, and all the animals, and the planet,
and you and Mrs. Obama too.

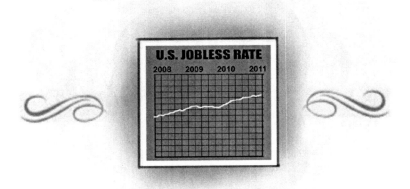

Ever wonder if he could be a Republican plant?

I *do* recognize the superior richness of her 1/4 Latina experience compared to
my white male imperialist background. I just don't see why that means
she gets my bedroom and I get the *couch.*

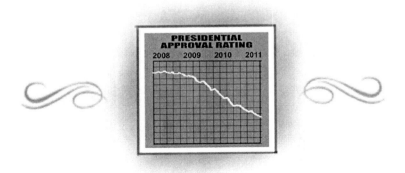

How soon before he labels this a crisis and pushes for
a government takeover of the Olympic Committee?

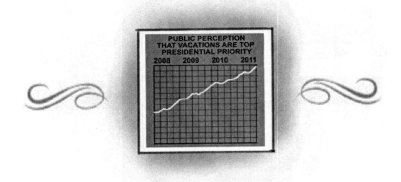

But that's exactly what I *hate* about common sense-- it's just so damn *common!*

Sure it's a bitch but all we gotta do is hang loose for a few months. Word has it our skill-sets totally qualify us for a sweet position in Government healthcare.

Very funny.

I love movies like that-- where gradually, bit by bit, all the characters start to realize that this super-cool guy they'd all staked their dreams on was really a total fake and a creepo.

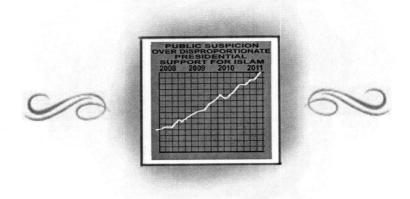

Oh thank goodness it's only *that*. I was terrified there'd be
some new global warming development.

I won't be a minute. Shabitha and the ACORN bunch are thinking they might
need to relocate and I told them I'd check out the new headquarters.

Wow, I see what you mean! But if ACORN is like a prostitute performing shady services for a 'client'-- the current, morally questionable administration-- in exchange for taxpayer money... who would ACORN's pimp be??

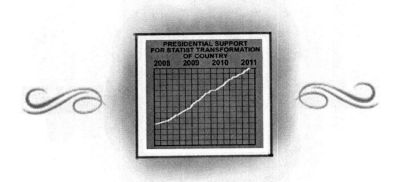

It's deadly, uncontainable and expanding like crazy. Think of it
as the ultimate metaphor for Obama's ego.

We know they're white; we know they go to church; we know he's a veteran.
If *you're* not ready to notify Homeland Security, *I* sure as hell am!

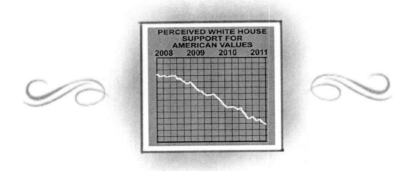

I don't think it means the dream is over. Do you think it means the dream is over?

When can we start looking for the Change to change back?

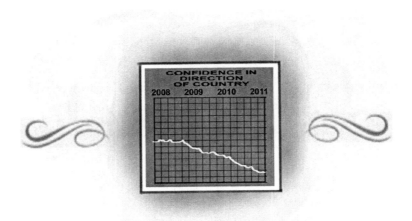

Y'know... maybe it's a *setting* sun, come to think of it.

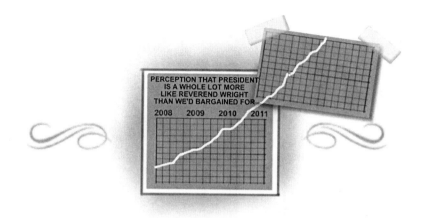

14.

STEP RIGHT UP!

...and they just set up these cheesy old tents this morning.
It's supposed to be some kind of revival show/vaudeville act...
real corny junk that nobody's seen around here like for *ever.*
C'mon, it'll be a hoot!

The *pla*net has a *fe*ver! Sweltering and burning... O, who will save us from the villainous manmade toxins as they turn our world to a ***burning pit of eternal hellfire??***

O, the *pity*...O, the heartbreak. *Look upon it my friends:* the *devastation* to all that is *Good* and *Green* at the hands of the **demonic SUV with its infernal toxins of carbon,** oh *believe*, my children, believe, for I speak the Green Word of Truth...

Damn you evil U.S. Industry! **Damn you** hellish U.S. Manufacturing! Manufacturing what? Goods for the people, you say? Valued commodities? *Or maybe Misery?* Maybe **Death?** And *rising CO² levels* that will **thrust** the **world** into an **eternal burning hell!!**

Run, I want to *run* from the pitiless heat that melts the icecap and drowns
all of Nature's wonders in a ***Rising Sea of Sorrow!*** But there is nowhere
to run my friends, and no-one to run from, for it's a sinful world and we are all sinners
and the name of that sin is ***Carbon Emissions!*** We have all
forsaken the Good and the Green have we not brothers and sisters?

Stand up, ye who share no blame in this sin!!

Turn we now my friends to a dramatic recitation by Devon.
Let us contemplate.

...and what did i find
when i sought sunlight and rainbows
and green green forests
in the forever meadows of Gaia?
i found man.
and in man i found darkness.
and i despaired of man and his factories,

man and his industries,
man and his metallic odes to work, fire & death.
where in this is joy?
where in this is sunlight?
where in this is rainbows
and green green forests
and the forever meadows of Gaia...

Ladies and gentleman, seek no farther than this very emporium for sunlight, joy and rainbows, for it is here! Look upon them, friends-- the Learned Professors, Learned Scientists and Learned Journalists, all in perfect unison, all singing and dancing as one in an identical lockstep to thrill your soul. *I give you..."The Global Warming Follies!"*

And now my friends we come to our answer, now we come to our **sal-vay-shun!** *I* would not leadeth you down a path of despair; the *Miraculous Green Elixir Capentrade* is the answer to all our fears, and it is *yours* for the Special Believers' Discount Price of just $258 a month per family for life oh *rejoice* my friends..! And the best part is-- you're already automatically signed on just for giving your name at the door when you entered the show, oh isn't it *wonderful* ladies & gentlemen? **Join! Hands! With your Neighbor!,** and ALL your neighbors across this great land, every last man, woman & child, who'll be receiving this miraculous green product all their lives long and thereby saving themselves from a **burning fate** too awful to mention.

But there's more! You'll also have the joy and satisfaction of knowing that while you do your duty by purchasing your monthly share of Capentrade, the filthy disgusting *corporations* that make our lives such a torment-- why, they'll be paying **thousands & thousands of times more than you will!** Ah, it's a glorious thing... *sing* with me now my friends!--

Living in the Green, living in the Green,
We shall go rejoicing, living in the Green!

Giving to the cause, writing brand new laws,
Capentrade forever, living in the Green!

Suddenly I feel sick... and broke!   Hey-- let's swing by that paddywagon
on the way out, maybe we can watch Professor Gorvel dispensing blessings
to the true believers.

A-hah! Just as I suspected! He's living in a *whole different kinda green*
than those folks back there at the tent show!

15.

THE SPRING/SUMMER/FALL/WINTER OF OUR DISCONTENT

Liking snow isn't racist, is it?

Yes... Alex? We were hiking on Mount Winnecowa and counselor Steve mentioned "God's country." How do you think this should be handled?

...Okay, how about this one: "Camp Guevara-- a planet-conscious,
socially aware Summer Experience Space combining
purposeful play with junior-level activism." Does that not sound *terrific?*

"...all campers are supplied with ethno-appropriate bracelets calibrated via Global Positioning System; monitor screens placed throughout the camp encourage children to seek out optimally diverse groups with whom to play. Diversity levels are further audited and maintained by camp counselors..."

"...gather round the environmentally sensitive campfire where we use only gas logs
(no wood or anything natural plays a role in any camp activities). We'll sing *Kumbaya*,
then analyze the words. Who is the "someone's crying" in Kumbaya? Could it be all of us?
Is *Blowin' in the Wind* a prophetic 1960s plea for wind power? We'll deconstruct *This Land is Your Land.*
Is it really "your land?" Is it really "my land?" What are the corporate powers that actually
own our land? How can we work to overturn..."

© 2008 by Zack Rawsthorne

Call them anything you want, just don't call them "snow angels."

*I wake up to find blatant hetero propaganda across the street
and I'm not supposed to be offended??*

Look, it's Barry Mobami-- the Smartest Kid in the Camp. Wouldn't you just love to listen in and hear what sort of fresh, new kernels of wisdom he's expounding on today?

But I don't *feel* like an 'oppressed minority crushed by a white corporate power-structure.' I feel like a kid having fun at summer camp!

Sure I'm up for it! *He'd* never steer us wrong.

This view isn't all that bad... but just imagine how incredible it would be if every tree were the same height with no inequality or size superiority, no tree overshadowed by any other, no tree bigger or better than its neighbor...

16.

UNHOLY HOLIDAYS
& OTHER PROGRESSIVE CELEBRATIONS

Her Moral Relativism Coming-Out Party. She's officially progressed
to the point where she's unable to make value judgments about *anything*.

Oh for chrissake. If you can't feel safe in Berkeley, where can you?

Thanks! Er... what is it?

Oh, like you know any *better* what we're supposed to do with it.

What could have gotten into her? It's too short to be a skirt,
too big to be a scarf, and isn't even in my colors!

It's Sierra-- she's been hospitalized. She moved into an endangered tree with some friends to kick off an Earth Day protest and lost her balance when they started clapping to 'Blowin' in the Wind.'

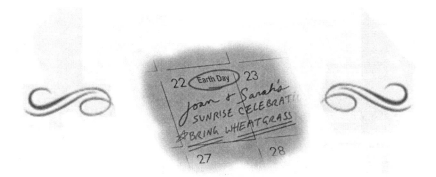

There's something about that face showing up at my doorstep with his hand open waiting for me to give him stuff that really creeps me out.

How do you know they're supposed to be zombies?
Maybe they're supposed to be Obama supporters.

It's the most politically correct Thanksgiving Day parade ever! They deflated
all the wildlife-offensive cartoon animals and sliced them up into "Coexist" ribbons!

Maybe that's what liberals need to combat Global Warming scepticism:
a compelling fantasy figure who flies magicaly through the sky rewarding
true believers and restoring childlike faith everywhere.

13

14 Che Guevara's
        Birthday

Karyn's
Party

ACORN
HEADQUARTERS?

20 New Moon
WARN
    SIERRA

21

Don't you hate it when people get you gifts that they like but you can't stand?

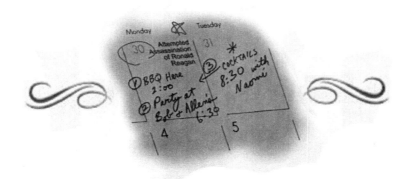

We *have* to go the long way. There's a Boy Scout troop selling Christmas trees from the church parking lot on Grant Street and she's convinced if she sees it she'll have a stroke.

END

BONUS! FREE "HYPNO-LEAFLET!"

YOU can help save America! The vast majority of liberal/leftists have sealed themselves off from common sense, but we can still try to reach them through their subconscious. Cut out this leaflet, make a bunch of copies and discreetly leave a couple laying around at chic coffeeshops, big city book stores, rock concerts and any other liberal hangouts you can think of. Consider sticking around to watch the results; if you're up to it, play dumb about the source of the flyer but answer their propaganda talking points with friendly, informed counterpoints. You just might have fun!

Increase Your Happiness & Wisdom Forever!

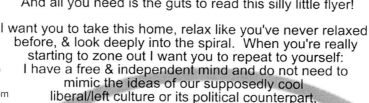

www.diversitylane.com

Listen up, because your life is about to change profoundly.
And all you need is the guts to read this silly little flyer!

I want you to take this home, relax like you've never relaxed before, & look deeply into the spiral. When you're really starting to zone out I want you to repeat to yourself:
I have a free & independent mind and do not need to mimic the ideas of our supposedly cool liberal/left culture or its political counterpart, the Democrat Party. I will summon up every scrap of guts and independence I have and give an experimental listen to so-called 'conservative talk radio' or Fox News for a few days in a row, at which point I will discover with shock & awe that they have an enormous amount of valuable information that I actually need to know in order to be an informed citizen, but which has mysteriously been kept from me until now. I will take on this bold thought-experiment even though the mainstream culture warns me not to listen because conservatives are evil, satanic and out to reinstitute slavery.

I will try to remember that America is an overwhelmingly benign nation where millions flock for a chance at freedom and prosperity impossible in virtually any other nation on earth. Every country has had war, conquest and lots of other rotten stuff tucked away in its history, and every country is flawed, so I will cease parroting the idiotic lie that our country is worse than others-- especially since none other has spread even a small fraction of the good will, wealth and lifesaving measures across the globe that America has. *This is not rah-rah jingoism; it's called: Being Honest.* I will forever keep this in mind despite what lots of my teachers, all of my professors, and about 99% of the mainstream media have tried to drum into me all my life.

I will begin to Question Authority when it comes to the mainstream culture including Hollywood, big New York and D.C. papers, the network news and all the rest of the popular but often wildly misinformed "journalists" and opinion-makers, whom I will soon realize have a biased, left-leaning take on the world which very often has nothing to do with reality.

I will read Animal Farm, study up on my history, and understand that people like Che & Fidel are/were bona fide murderers, confiscating thieves and nation-destroyers, not good dudes; that, check it out, socialism, marxism & communism have been the greatest cause of bloodshed & human misery in the history of the planet; and that gigantic, expanded government is closely related to them. It's like the biggest conceivable big business, & the bigger it gets, the more impersonal & inhuman it gets. There is nothing even remotely positive about any of these systems. If I advocate for them it means I am a dupe who has been fooled by ignorant & ahistorical elites, foreign & domestic, who've been peddling a load of dangerous (though *chic*) bull to the public for a good 50 years or more.

And, I will never again vote for a candidate because happening celebs, my friends, and other cool people say I should-- especially if there is documented proof that the candidate has associates, mentors and/or ministers who are obviously hate-filled bigots or who have bombed the Capitol & the Pentagon.

More at www.diversitylane.com & www.diversitylane.wordpress.com

LaVergne, TN USA
27 January 2011
214316LV00001B/2/P